DiVE INTO THE DEEP

Written and Illustrated by

lulu's
LITTLE
LIBRARY

WELCOME TO THE WONDERFUL KINGDOM BENEATH THE WAVES, WHERE THE SECRETS OF THE UNDERWATER WORLD COME ALIVE IN A SYMPHONY OF COLOR AND PLAYFUL WONDER. WITH EACH TURN OF THE PAGE, YOU'LL MEET A FASCINATING NEW CREATURE, EACH WITH ITS OWN STORY TO TELL. SO TAKE A DEEP BREATH, DIVE INTO THE DEPTHS, AND PREPARE TO BE AMAZED.

CLICK, CLICK!
I'M FLIPPER, THE PLAYFUL DOLPHIN.

CLICK
CLICK

I SWIM GRACEFULLY THROUGH THE OCEAN, LEAPING AND TWIRLING.
MY SLEEK BODY AND FRIENDLY CLICKS BRING JOY TO ALL.

SLOW AND STEADY WiNS THE RACE!
I'M SHELLY, THE WiSE TURTLE.

I GLIDE THROUGH THE WATER, CARRYING MY COZY SHELL ON MY BACK. I'VE EXPLORED THE OCEAN FOR MANY YEARS, AND I'M A SYMBOL OF WISDOM AND PATIENCE.

NEiGH, NEiGH! WAiT, THAT'S NOT RIGHT!
I'M SEBASTiAN, THE GRACEFUL SEAHORSE.

WITH MY CURVY BODY AND DELICATE FINS, I NAVIGATE THE VIBRANT CORAL REEFS WITH ELEGANCE. I CAMOUFLAGE MYSELF AMONG THE COLORFUL CORALS, SWAYING GENTLY WITH THE CURRENTS.

WIGGLE, WIGGLE!
I'M OSCAR, THE CLEVER OCTOPUS.

WIGGLE
WIGGLE
WIGGLE

WITH MY EIGHT ARMS, I EXPLORE THE NOOKS AND CRANNIES OF THE OCEAN FLOOR. I'M A MASTER OF DISGUISE, CHANGING COLORS AND SHAPES.

HELLO, GUYS!
I AM CORI, THE JOLLY CLOWN FISH.

GIGGLE

GIGGLE

GIGGLE

I LIVE AMONG THE SWAYING ANEMONES, WHICH ARE MY HOME AND PROTECTOR. WITH MY VIBRANT COLORS AND PLAYFUL PERSONALITY, I BRING SMILES TO ALL WHO SEE ME.

DUN DUN, DUN DUN!
WATCH OUT, IT'S SHARKY, THE MIGHTY SHARK!

I'M RULING THE DEPTHS OF THE OCEAN. WITH MY SHARP TEETH AND POWERFUL BODY, I ENSURE THE BALANCE OF THE MARINE ECOSYSTEM.

SPARKLE, SPARKLE!
I'M CHROMA, THE BRILLIANT RAINBOWFISH.

MY SCALES SHIMMER WITH ALL THE COLORS OF THE RAINBOW. I DART THROUGH THE CORAL REEFS, SPREADING JOY WITH MY VIBRANT PRESENCE.

FLOAT, FLOAT!
I'M JASPER, THE ETHEREAL JELLYFISH.

I DRIFT THROUGH THE WATER, WITH LONG TENTACLES. WITH MY ENTRANCING BIOLUMINESCENT GLOW, I BRING CHARM TO THE DEEP SEA.

WHOOSH, WHOOSH!
I'M MANDY, THE GRACIOUS MANTA RAY.

I GLIDE THROUGH THE WATER, MY WINGS GENTLY FLAPPING.
I'M KNOWN FOR MY MAJESTIC SIZE AND FRIENDLY NATURE.

BARK, BARK!
I'M LEO, THE PLAYFUL SEA LION.

BARK
BARK

I BASK ON ROCKY SHORES AND DIVE INTO THE OCEAN WITH GRACE. WITH MY ACROBATIC FLIPS AND PLAYFUL NATURE, I ENTERTAIN BOTH ABOVE AND BELOW THE SURFACE.

TWINKLE, TWINKLE!
I'M SANDY, THE RADIANT STARFISH.

TWINKLE TWINKLE

I DWELL PEACEFULLY ON THE SANDY OCEAN FLOOR, MY DELICATE ARMS REACHING OUT IN EVERY DIRECTION. I EMBODY THE MARVEL OF REGENERATION AND THE BEAUTY OF THE UNDERWATER WORLD.

ZOOM, ZOOM!
I'M FINN, THE ADVENTUROUS FLYING FISH.

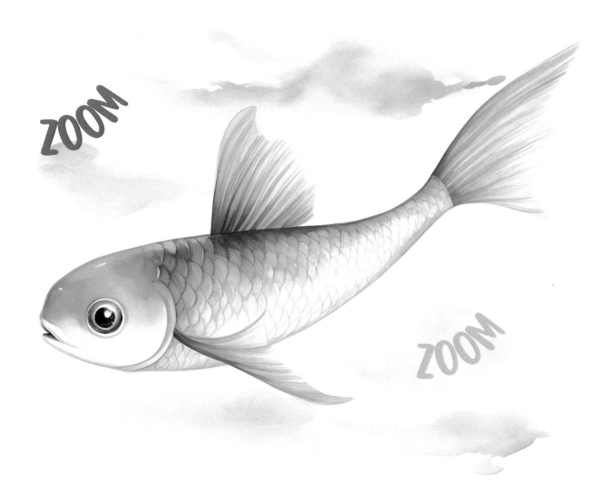

I GLIDE ABOVE THE WATER'S SURFACE, USING MY LONG FINS TO CATCH THE WIND. I'M KNOWN FOR MY INCREDIBLE LEAPS AND ABILITY TO SOAR THROUGH THE AIR.

SPLASH, SPLASH!
I'M OSCAR, THE INTELLIGENT ORCA.

SPLASH

I'M A MAJESTIC PREDATOR, SWIMMING IN PODS WITH MY FAMILY.
WITH MY SLEEK BLACK AND WHITE BODY, I NAVIGATE THE OCEAN
WITH PRECISION.

WHiSTLE, WHiSTLE!
I'M MARiNA, THE GENTLE MANATEE.

WHiSTLE

I LIVE IN CALM COASTAL WATERS, GRAZING QUIETLY ON PLANTS. WITH MY SLOW MOVEMENTS AND FRIENDLY ATTITUDE, I BRING PEACE TO THE OCEAN.

WADDLE, WADDLE!
I'M PERCY, THE ADORABLE PENGUIN.

ALTHOUGH I SPEND MOST OF MY TIME IN ICY WATERS, I OCCASIONALLY DIVE INTO THE OCEAN. WITH MY SLEEK FEATHERS AND CHARMING PERSONALITY, I BRING JOY TO ALL WHO ENCOUNTER ME.

FLUTTER, FLUTTER!
I'M BUTTERCUP, THE COLORFUL BUTTERFLYFISH.

FLUTTER

I NAVIGATE THROUGH CORAL REEFS, SHOWCASING MY VIBRANT PATTERNS AND FLUTTERING FINS. I BRING A TOUCH OF ELEGANCE TO THE UNDERWATER WORLD.

SWISH, SWISH!
I'M SYLVIA, THE SWIFT SWORDFISH.

WITH MY LONG, SHARP BILL, I SWIFTLY NAVIGATE THROUGH THE OPEN OCEAN. I'M A SKILLED HUNTER, USING MY SPEED AND AGILITY TO CATCH MY PREY.

GLITTER, SHIMMER!
I'M GOLDIE, THE SHIMMERING GOLDFISH.

GLITTER

SHIMMER

IN TRANQUIL PONDS AND LAKES, I MAKE MY HOME AND I SPREAD JOY WITH EACH GRACEFUL SWIM. MY GOLDEN SCALES SHIMMER, CASTING A MAGICAL GLOW.

ROAR, ROAR!
I'M WALLY, THE MAJESTIC WALRUS.

I CALL THE ARCTIC WATERS MY HOME, BALANCING ON ICY PLATFORMS AND DIVING FOR TREATS. WITH MY BIG, BLUBBERY BODY AND FRIENDLY SMILE, I BRING LAUGHTER AND JOY TO THE FROZEN WORLD.

PUFF, PUFF!
I'M PUFFY, THE ADORABLE PUFFERFISH.

I HAVE THE UNIQUE ABILITY TO PUFF UP WHEN THREATENED, TURNING INTO A SPIKY BALL. I'M KNOWN FOR MY COMICAL APPEARANCE AND DEFENSIVE TACTICS.

Made in the USA
Middletown, DE
19 November 2024

65038766R00027